This is a fictionalised biography describing some
of the key moments (so far!) in the career of
Kylian Mbappé.
Some of the events described in this book are
based upon the author's imagination and are
probably not entirely accurate representations
of what actually happened.

Tales from the Pitch
Kylian Mbappé
by Harry Coninx

Published by Raven Books
An imprint of Ransom Publishing Ltd.
Unit 7, Brocklands Farm, West Meon, Hampshire GU32 1JN, UK
www.ransom.co.uk

ISBN   978 178591 975 6
First published in 2020
Reprinted 2021 (three times)

There is a reading comprehension quiz available for this book in the popular
Accelerated Reader® software system. For information about ATOS, Accelerated
Reader, quiz points and reading levels please visit www.renaissance.com. Accelerated
Reader, AR, the Accelerated Reader Logo, and ATOS are trademarks of Renaissance
Learning, Inc. and its subsidiaries, registered common law or applied for in the U.S.
and other countries. Used under license.

TALES FROM THE PITCH

KYLIAN MBAPPÉ

HARRY CONINX

RAVEN

For my dad, and all our years of Hall Football

CONTENTS

I

CHAMPIONS OF THE WORLD

July 2018, Luzhniki Stadium, Moscow, Russia
World Cup Final, France v Croatia

The French team sat silently and listened as a low rumble of thunder merged with the noise of the crowd outside.

It wasn't usually this tense before a game, but most of these players had been at the Euros two years ago, when France had been beaten in the final by Portugal.

That had been a huge loss, and those in the French

team who'd played in that game were still haunted by their performance on that day.

But not all the players had been there.

Kylian, for one, had only watched the game on TV. He'd been seventeen then and seeing Portugal celebrate that win had crushed him.

He'd already set his mind on getting into the French squad for the World Cup in Russia, and seeing that loss had made him all the more determined to be where he was right now. He wasn't going to sit by and risk another trophy slipping away.

"Come on, lads! Let's get going!"

The shout from Hugo Lloris stirred the team into action. Kylian leapt to his feet and followed the pack of players to the door.

Opposite them, the Croatian team were emerging from their dressing room. As Kylian watched, Ivan Rakitić, Luka Modrić and Mario Mandžukić strode past him. There were some big names in that team – players who had already won many major trophies.

The words of the French manager Didier Deschamps played over and over in Kylian's head.

"Kylian, you're quicker than every player on that team by a mile. You start running at them and they'll panic."

The day was overcast and the air was damp. It wasn't typical World Cup weather, but this suited Kylian down to the ground. The wetter the turf, the more likely a defender was to slip.

And as soon as a defender slipped, Kylian would be there to pounce.

The national anthems of France and Croatia rang out across the stadium. Both teams sang with passion, each player incredibly proud to be representing their country.

"It's a good thing you're a better footballer than you are a singer, Kylian," Antoine Griezmann quietly teased when *La Marseillaise* had come to an end.

Kylian smiled back at him wickedly, then began to make his way to his starting position.

Moments later, the game was underway.

Kylian got a few early touches and at every opportunity began running at the Croatian defence, just as his manager had instructed.

Kylian trusted Didier wholeheartedly and he wanted

to show him that his confidence in such a young player wasn't misplaced. Kylian also knew he was made for this level of football – made for winning the World Cup for his country.

Twenty minutes in and he found himself lining up in the Croatian box. France had been awarded a free kick.

Griezmann floated the ball over and several blue shirts flew into the air. It deflected off somebody and spun into the top corner.

GOAL!

Several French players wheeled away in celebration, turning to face the French fans.

"Raph, was that you?" Kylian shouted at Raphaël Varane, as he sprinted after his team-mate.

"Nah, I thought it was Olivier!" Varane responded, gesturing to Olivier Giroud.

It turned out that the ball had actually bounced off the head of Mario Mandžukić, the Croatian striker.

But the celebrations were cut short when shortly afterwards Ivan Perišić slammed the ball into the back of the French net. The red-and-white half of the stadium erupted noisily, drowning out the French fans.

Kylian frowned. The last thing they needed was the Croatian team being encouraged by plenty of vocal support from their fans.

"Let's keep them quiet, lads!" Paul Pogba bellowed.

As the game stuttered towards half-time, a French corner was followed by a heated appeal for handball.

"Penalty! Kylian, did you see that?" Samuel Umtiti screamed, waving his arms in the air.

Kylian turned to the referee, expecting to see him waving away the players' appeals, but instead he was gesturing to his ear. They were going to check the video replays.

"What do you think, Olivier? Did you see it?" Kylian asked his strike partner.

"It all happened so fast, I've got no idea, mate," Giroud replied with a shrug.

After what seemed like hours, the referee came away from the screen and signalled for a penalty.

"Come on, lads!" Kylian shouted.

Griezmann stepped up and slotted it away into the bottom left corner, making it 2-1 to France.

The half-time break took far too long for Kylian. As always, he was itching to get back out on to the pitch.

He was always thrilled for his team-mates when they scored, but he still wanted one for himself. One that would plaster his name across the history books.

Soon he was back out there, running into space and screaming for the ball.

"Paul! Now!"

Pogba obediently fired the ball into the gap and Kylian sprinted after it, beating the Croatian defenders.

As they regrouped he took them on, effortlessly holding the ball up until his team-mates could join him.

He fed it through to Griezmann, who quickly slipped it back to Pogba.

GOAL!

Kylian raised his arms into the air.

Pogba had made it 3-1!

It felt as if they already had one hand on the World Cup trophy. But they couldn't afford to lose their momentum.

Only a few minutes later and Lucas Hernandez was driving forward yet again, looking for a pass. Kylian's instincts kicked in and he sprinted towards him.

"Lucas! Over here!"

The ball skimmed over the turf to Kylian's feet. What followed felt so natural.

With the first touch he got the ball out from under his feet and with the second he fired it from 25 yards, straight past the keeper and into the bottom corner.

GOAL!

Adrenaline surged through him as the ball hit home. He'd scored in a World Cup final! So sweet! It was what he'd spent his whole childhood dreaming about – and the rest of his life practising for.

He jogged over to the French fans and took up his traditional cross-armed celebration. The fans had just a second to see it, before the entire French team piled on top of him.

"You legend!" Griezmann yelled into his ear. "I swear, the only teenager who's ever scored in a World Cup final before was – Pele!"

A late goal from Croatia wasn't enough and the final

whistle soon sounded, confirming France's victory.

They were officially World Cup champions – the best team in the world.

The scene erupted into madness. Kylian could feel people jumping on him and kissing his head.

Somebody even shoved their phone under his nose, and in all the chaos he managed to read what was on the screen:

@Pele

Welcome to the club, @KMbappe – it's great to have some company!

"Remember this moment, lads!" Deschamps shouted as the team huddled together on the pitch. "It doesn't get better than this!"

Kylian beamed at the manager who'd given him this chance. But quietly, Kylian disagreed.

It *would* get better than this.

He'd *always* planned on doing better, and he had his whole career ahead of him to make that happen.

2

MORE OF A PLAYER

July 2006

Kylian's childhood home, Bondy, Paris, France

"KYLIAN! Come on!" A seven-year-old Kylian glanced up at the window the shout had come from, then decided to ignore it. He carried on dribbling the ball, then fired a shot at the brick wall outside his apartment block.

"GOAALLL!!" he shouted, wheeling away in celebration, picturing the fans springing to their feet and cheering his name.

"Kylian! Get in here! Quickly!" his dad shouted again. "The game's about to start!"

This time, Kylian turned and sprinted into the block, racing up the stairs that led to his apartment. Today was going to be huge … France were playing Italy in the World Cup final.

He burst into the living room where his family and a group of neighbours were gathered around the TV.

Shuffling his way into the centre, he sat at his dad's feet with his legs tightly crossed.

Wilfried was thrilled to have his son finally in the room. He'd been calling Kylian in for about half an hour, much to the amusement of his guests.

"He's more of a player than a watcher," Wilfried explained to them with a chuckle.

But there was no need to explain. Bondy was a tight-knit community and everyone in the town knew that Kylian was football-mad. It was common knowledge that he was already incredibly talented too.

"So, what do you think, Kylian? France for the win, is it?" Wilfried said, as he gently shook him by the shoulders.

"Obviously!" Kylian replied, without hesitation.

The first 10 minutes of the game were tense, and Kylian's attention was already starting to fade.

He'd really been looking forward to watching the game, but now that he was here he was just itching to get back outside and make the most of the light summer evening.

His mind had drifted off to thoughts about practising his passing, when he heard everybody in the room cheer. The noise pulled him back to the game on the TV.

"Kylian, look! A penalty!" his dad shouted as he punched the air.

Florent Malouda had been brought down in the box and the French captain, Zinedine Zidane, was stepping up to take it.

The ball went straight down the middle, slamming against the bar and bouncing down.

"Was that in?" Kylian shouted, jumping to his feet with excitement.

They all waited for what seemed like hours while the ref made his decision.

It was a goal!

Kylian joined his father and the neighbours in the celebrations.

But only minutes later Italy were back level.

The tense match played on and, again, Kylian struggled to keep his attention on the game. For him, the only high points were when Thierry Henry got on the ball.

"Look at him run, Dad! The defenders can't get near him!" Kylian shouted every time Henry picked up the ball.

"Watch him now, Kylian," his dad whispered. "Watch what he does when he doesn't have the ball. Look at how he makes space for himself, away from the defenders."

Kylian nodded. His dad – who was also the coach at AS Bondy, the local club where Kylian played – gave the best football advice in the world. Whether it was Ligue One predictions, tactics, or tips, there was nobody Kylian trusted more.

So he did as he said and tried to focus on Henry's movement, though really it just made him want to be back outside, practising his own running.

Meanwhile the match ground on, with both teams struggling to make any goals happen.

"When is there going to be another goal, Dad?" Kylian moaned.

"If you want goals, Kylian, you'll have to become a player and get out there yourself!"

It was still 1-1 after 90 minutes, so the game continued to extra time, but Kylian was sent to bed well before the end.

Worn out by his day of football outside the apartment, he quickly drifted off to sleep, undisturbed by the noise of the adults still sitting downstairs.

His dreams that night were more vivid than usual. He dreamt that he was up front with Henry, for France, and then he was lifting the World Cup trophy for his country.

It all seemed so real that, when he woke up, it took him a moment to adjust to being in his bedroom and not in a stadium full of cheering fans.

Once he was fully awake, he reached straight for the football that he'd placed safely by the side of his bed and shot downstairs.

"Dad! Dad!" he yelled, as he scooted round the house looking for his father. "Did we win?"

Wilfried was sitting at the kitchen table, sipping his coffee and flicking through the morning paper.

He looked up as his son came flying into the room and gave him a sad little smile.

He held up the paper and gestured at the headline.

ITALY ARE
WORLD CHAMPIONS

"Sorry, son," he said. "Zidane lost his head and got sent off. Then Italy won on penalties. We were really unlucky."

Kylian looked at his disappointed father's face, then sighed, turned on his heels and started to head outside.

"Hey! Hey, Kylian!" his dad called after him. "You should have some breakfast!"

"I'm not going to help us win the World Cup by eating breakfast, Dad!" Kylian shouted back.

He was already half-way down the road, booting the ball up into the air.

3
CHELSEA'S CHANCE

March 2011
Clairefontaine Academy, Paris

Some days, Kylian still had to pinch himself. Yes, he really *was* at a school for footballers.

He remembered the day he found out he'd been accepted, just as if it was yesterday.

"Kylian, have you ever heard of Clairefontaine?" his dad had asked him.

"Nah," Kylian had replied, without much interest.

"Who is he? Does he play for Marseille?"

Looking back, Kylian still wanted to cringe at how stupid he must have seemed. He could still remember his dad trying to hold back his smile while he explained to his son that Clairefontaine was actually a very famous school.

"A school?" Kylian had replied with disgust. "A *school*? Why would I care about a school?"

"Because it's a school for footballers. *Just* footballers. Thierry Henry went there, and Anelka, too!"

Wilfried paused to let that sink in.

"Well, together with the other coaches at Bondy, I put you forward, a while back. I know, I should have told you. But … well, only the very best get in, and … "

Another pause.

" … they want you, Kylian!"

Now, a few months into training at Clairefontaine Academy, treading in the footsteps of his heroes, Kylian's football was going from strength to strength.

He'd loved playing for AS Bondy and he missed

having his dad as the team coach, but he knew in his heart that it had never really been challenging enough for him.

Even when they'd realised that he was *way* better than the other kids his own age, and they'd let him play in the older team, he'd still found it easy.

He'd never had to try very hard, and that had meant he'd not really been developing as a player.

At Clairefontaine he was being challenged and he came to every training session knowing that he was going to leave it a better player – a player a little more like one of his heroes.

And since the school was in Paris, he could carry on living at home with his parents.

It felt like a win-win. He loved being around boys who could play football at his level, and he loved learning the game from world-class coaches.

But he still had his life at home. Home was a bolthole, somewhere he could go where there was no pressure and where he could have a ball at his feet without feeling as if anyone was judging him.

As he skipped out on to the Clairefontaine pitch

today, he noticed there was a different kind of buzz in the air.

There were some smartly dressed men who Kylian didn't recognise scattered around the sidelines, furiously scribbling into little notebooks.

One of the coaches noticed Kylian staring at the group of men, so he went over and crouched down next to him.

"You see that guy there," he said, gesturing to one of the men. "He's from Real Madrid."

Kylian looked across, mouth open wide, but the coach hadn't finished.

"That guy – he's from Liverpool."

He went on, pointing out the scouts who were representing some of Europe's biggest clubs.

"They're not all here for *me*, are they?" Kylian mumbled, slightly taken aback.

"Pretty much, Kylian," his coach smiled. "Try not to worry about them, though. Just enjoy the game."

It was an anxious wait after the match was over.

Kylian felt as if it had been one of the best games of his life. He'd scored twice and had set up two other goals, but he still couldn't shake the feeling that he hadn't done enough.

He stood and stared at the scouts for what felt like hours, willing them to come over and tell him he was exactly what they were looking for.

As they eventually all turned and started to walk away, Kylian ran over to the coach who'd told him who was who.

"Hey, Kylian," the coach said reassuringly. "They're not going to make a decision straight away. It doesn't work like that. You might hear something in a few days, or weeks – or even months. But you just have to carry on. Stay focused on your football."

It wasn't advice Kylian was going to take on board easily. His mind was racing at the thought of playing for the clubs he adored – playing alongside his heroes.

"What if Real Madrid offer me a deal, Dad? Will we move to Madrid? Will I need to learn Spanish? I might meet Ronaldo!"

Wilfried couldn't help but be touched by his son's enthusiasm.

He was just as excited for Kylian, though he was trying to lead by example and not get too carried away himself.

It was always a struggle to play all his roles in Kylian's life properly. As Kylian's coach, he needed to build him up and give him confidence in his abilities. But as a parent, he needed to keep his son's feet on the ground.

And now, as Kylian's agent as well, he would need to have his back and answer the many questions Kylian had, even when he'd heard the same questions every night for the last week.

Then, every night, after Kylian had gone to bed, his mother would also ask Wilfried if there had been any news that day.

Fayza was a sportswoman herself and she had always been adamant that Kylian was going to be a sporting star, ever since she'd felt his first kick in the womb during her pregnancy.

"No, no news yet," Wilfried would reply with a laugh. "You know, you're nearly as bad as Kylian!"

Eventually, a call did come through, but it wasn't from Real Madrid.

Kylian bounced into the kitchen one day, after a long training session, to find his dad sitting at the kitchen table.

Kylian was about to tell him all about the footwork he'd been practising, when he registered the excited smile on his dad's face.

"Is it an offer?" Kylian asked quickly.

"Yes," his dad said, still grinning.

"Well?" Kylian shouted. "Who is it?"

His dad paused for what seemed like an eternity. "It's Chelsea."

Kylian's mouth fell open. Chelsea wasn't his favourite club, but they were still huge and just the fact that they were offering him a trial was insane.

He shot straight up the stairs to pack his suitcase, ignoring his mum and dad's shouts that they wouldn't be leaving for England for another week.

Kylian looked up eagerly at the Chelsea official who was taking him to the training ground, where he was due to play a match in Chelsea's youth team.

"Are we going to meet Frank Lampard?" Kylian babbled excitedly. It was an important question and he'd taken the time to learn it in English.

"Not today, kid," the man replied dryly.

Before he knew it, Kylian was pulling the shirt he'd been given over his head and was lining up alongside the rest of the Chelsea players.

His chattiness was cut dead as it struck him that he didn't know any of these other kids, and his English wasn't good enough for him to be able to talk to them properly.

Nonetheless he tried as hard as he could in the game, but he struggled to get the ball. He could feel that he was out of position a lot, and he knew that his poor English – together with his accent – wasn't making things easier.

Kylian knew that he wasn't playing at his best, but by the time the match was over he wasn't sure that England was right for him anyway.

At least, not yet.

It seemed that the coaches agreed and after the game, as soon as they were sitting down with the Mbappé family, they explained that they wouldn't be making an offer.

"We still think he has something about him," one of the translators for the Chelsea officials went on, "and we know that everyone has bad days. So we would like to invite him back for a second trial."

Kylian was ready to tell them that wasn't what he wanted but, before he could say anything, his mum was speaking.

"Either you sign him now, or within five years you'll have to offer 50 million Euro to tie him down," she told the officials.

She hadn't shouted or lost her temper as she'd spoken – rather, she'd told them softly but very clearly.

She meant it and she wanted them to know it.

The translator politely refused her deal on behalf of the club.

"You're going to be snapped up soon, Kylian. Just you wait and see," his mum told him, as they packed up their things back at the hotel.

She was trying to make sure that her son wasn't upset by the events of the day, but there was no need. Kylian knew that Chelsea wasn't the best place for him right now, and he was already looking forward to being back home and getting stuck into his training.

4
SNAPPED UP

November 2015
Monaco training ground, Monaco

It was surreal being at Monaco, but Kylian had known straight away that it was the right place for him. After all, this had been Thierry Henry's club.

But that hadn't made his first year there any easier.

He'd been only fourteen when he joined the club and he'd desperately missed home. His dad in particular had always been totally involved in Kylian's life and his football, so getting on without his dad's regular guidance and reassurance was tough.

There were many evenings when Kylian just wanted to be able to chat with his dad about what had happened that day in training.

Whenever the Monaco first team played, Kylian thought of sitting with his dad in the living room back home, watching the game on the TV with him, getting excited together about where Kylian would one day fit in with the team.

But instead he had to make do with lying on his bed in the Monaco dorm, eyes closed, pretending he was back in his bedroom at home – surrounded by all his football posters, hearing his dad milling about in the room next door and hearing people walking along the familiar streets outside.

For all that, it didn't occur to Kylian to leave Monaco. For one, he was really enjoying the football there.

But more important, he knew that this was what he *had* to do to become as good as his heroes, the players on those posters on his bedroom walls – the likes of Ronaldo, Zidane and Henry.

And then, at some point, without realizing exactly when it happened, Kylian started to think of Monaco as his second home.

The coaches for the Monaco youth team were certainly pleased by his arrival. When Kylian first arrived, he quickly found that his crossing and dribbling abilities were already far superior to those of his team-mates.

But something else had been bitingly clear to his coaches. Kylian was *quick*.

Speed in itself wasn't unusual – many players were quick – but quick players were usually smaller and therefore prone to getting knocked around by defenders and losing possession.

But Kylian was naturally well-built. He was quick *and* strong – a deadly combination – so there was no knocking him off the ball, even if you could catch up with him. In fact, once Kylian had flicked the ball past a defender, a chance on goal was a sure thing.

But Kylian did sometimes struggle when he was

one-on-one with a keeper. In those situations he'd sometimes miss the target, scuffing the ball wide.

Kylian had become aware of this and had already tried a few different techniques – placing his shots into the corners, chipping the keeper and even going round him, but all without much success.

Kylian was beginning to feel he was running out of options. After all, finishing was so important – he *had* to crack it.

One of the coaches had quickly spotted his difficulties and set about helping him.

"I used to go for power," the coach calmly explained. "If you're ever in doubt, put your foot through it. The pace is normally enough to beat the keeper."

Kylian was grateful for any advice, but at this a flash of disappointment crossed his face – somehow he'd hoped for something more.

"I know. It's not much, is it?" The coach smiled as he saw Kylian's expression. "But football is a simple game sometimes. Just try it."

In the next reserve match Kylian was, as usual, a class above the other players. Every touch he made was immense and he was pulling out skill after skill. Then suddenly, after a fast ball in to his feet that he flicked between the legs of a defender, he found himself one-on-one with the keeper.

He had time to think about what to do. At first he eyed up the corner, but then he remembered his coach's advice, so he just smashed it, clean and hard. The ball flew through the air and smacked the back of the net. Kylian turned to the sideline and spotted the coach who had given him the tip.

He gave Kylian a big thumbs-up, then started making circles with his hands – he wanted to see it again.

And Kylian delivered. Two more goals followed in that match and from then on, any time the ball fell to him in a tough position, he just went for power.

It was just one of the many lessons that had propelled him to where he was now, training with the first team, kicking a ball with players like Bernardo Silva, João Moutinho and Fabinho.

Monaco were building a squad filled with young players who were capable of challenging the one team that had dominated the French league for many years – PSG. There was a strong atmosphere of belief around the Monaco team, and Kylian was thrilled to be a part of it.

"You're five times the player I was at sixteen!" João said to him, after he'd curled a shot into the top corner, straight past the keeper, Subašić.

He was just turning to João to thank him when he was interrupted by the sound of his name being shouted across the pitch.

It was Leonardo Jardim, Monaco's manager, who was calling him. So Kylian jogged over to where he was standing, alongside another important-looking man.

"Kylian, this is Vadim. He's the vice president of the club." Then Leonardo turned to Vadim and continued. "This is Kylian. He's one of our brightest stars."

Kylian glanced at both men. Not many players were being introduced to the vice president of their club at the age of sixteen, and he wasn't entirely sure where this was all going.

"Look, Kylian, I know you've been pressing for a chance in the first team, and I want to give it to you," Leonardo said, smiling at Kylian and Vadim.

Leonardo carried on talking, but his words were now falling on deaf ears. Kylian had stopped listening. That one sentence had made all those long nights missing home when he'd first moved here worthwhile. His chance had come. He was going to be out on the pitch, soaking up the atmosphere of a match as part of Monaco's first team!

When he tuned back into the conversation, it was Vadim speaking.

" … And in a few months, the plan is to offer you your first professional contract," he said. "Hopefully, it will be a contract you like."

"Yes. Absolutely. Definitely. I know it will," Kylian babbled.

"Well, maybe let your agent look at it first," Leonardo laughed. "It's still your father, right?"

Kylian nodded furiously. He was just itching to get away and tell his father the news.

As soon as he had the chance Kylian rang home and asked to be put on the speaker, so he could tell both his parents at the same time.

For a second, they didn't say anything. They just exchanged glances, trying to work out if their son was just messing with them for the amusement of his younger brother, Ethan.

"But if you play on Saturday, Kylian, you'll be the youngest player for Monaco – *ever!*' his dad said breathlessly.

"You bet!" Kylian shouted. As he listened to his mum's praise about how she always knew he would do great things, he could hear his dad in the background, tapping away on the keyboard of a laptop.

"Kylian!" he heard his dad gasp. "Guess who *was* Monaco's youngest player, before you?"

"I don't know, dad. Who?"

"Thierry Henry!" his dad exclaimed. "That's whose record you'll be taking!"

5

HENRY WHO?

December 2015
Stade Louis II Stadium, Monaco

The club were good on their word and the team sheet that Friday included the one name Kylian was desperate to see. His own.

33 MBAPPÉ

Come Saturday he was on the bus, chatting with Bernardo as they headed for their game against SM Caen.

The crowd wasn't the biggest Monaco had seen, but to Kylian it was huge, and it took him a while to spot his parents in the stands, even though he knew where they'd be sitting.

He also knew his dad would have everyone in Bondy watching on their TVs, and he was excited to show them how far he'd already come.

The game kicked off and, as he'd expected, he started on the bench.

The first sub was Hélder Costa and then Elderson Echiéjilé was called up, while Kylian remained stuck in his seat.

He kept glancing up at the scoreboard, checking the time. Maybe they'd forgotten their promise, or there'd been a change of plan.

But then, with two minutes left on the clock, it was his turn.

Kylian pulled up his socks as Fábio Coentrão came off. Sprinting onto the pitch, he immediately called for the ball and got his first few touches. It was exhilarating and he already felt addicted, just being out there.

A few minutes later, when full time rolled around, Bernardo bounded over to him.

"So, how'd you find it?" he asked, as he wrapped his arm around Kylian.

"Insane. I loved it. But I'm really hoping for a start next time," Kylian replied.

Bernardo raised his eyebrows at his team-mate's ambition but, after a thoughtful pause, he nodded and said it was probably only a matter of time.

Two weeks later, Kylian had made his first start – in a cup game, away against Bordeaux.

He'd enjoyed all 90 minutes and had felt really at home on the pitch, but mentally he'd already moved on. He was in a hurry for the next thing. Now he wanted to make an impact on the game – he wanted a goal.

Back in training, he was working on just that when Leonardo pulled him aside.

"Kylian, where do you want to play?" he asked.

Kylian was a little taken aback and didn't really know what to say.

"Striker?" he replied, sounding a little unsure.

"Yeah, that's what I thought," Leonardo said.

He paused for a moment before continuing. "One of your heroes is Henry, right?"

Kylian nodded.

"I assume you know he started out as a left winger, don't you?"

Kylian nodded again.

"Well, that's where I see you. You're quick, you're an incredible dribbler and you have a lot of skill. I want you out wide, able to move inside to finish when the moment's right. How does that sound?"

Kylian looked at Leonardo, feeling a little unsure.

All the years he'd spent dreaming about being a footballer, he'd only ever imagined himself as a striker.

It was the best position – you get lots of the ball, you get to run at people and you get to have a cool celebration.

Then another thought occurred to him.

Cristiano Ronaldo, his other favourite player, had started out on the left wing too. So it couldn't be *that* bad.

And besides, Kylian was quietly confident that he could score goals wherever he played.

"Sure, I can do that!" he said enthusiastically.

"Just get out there and tire them out!" Leonardo told Kylian, as he jumped up and down on the touchline. "And if it falls to you, don't be afraid to pull the trigger and have a shot!"

Kylian certainly wasn't afraid to have a shot. It was what he'd been trying to do for his last few games, but he hadn't quite managed it yet.

Now, going on for these last 20 minutes against Troyes AC, he wanted to make it happen.

Out on the pitch, he could sense some of the nerves in the Monaco team. Troyes had pulled a goal back, making the score 2-1 to Monaco. They needed another one to kill the game.

Suddenly Hélder Costa burst forward. Kylian could see some space, so he sprinted forward to support his team-mate, overtaking several defenders.

"Hélder! Pull it back!" he screamed.

Hélder dragged it back and the ball came to Kylian. He swung at it hard with his left foot and it landed in the back of the net.

GOAL!

Kylian raised his arms and turned towards the fans. They were on their feet, cheering wildly. Kylian knew that scoring for the first team would feel amazing, but this was better than he'd imagined.

The full-time whistle came seconds later and Kylian was beaming as several of his team-mates came over and hugged him.

"I don't think I'd even played a professional game at the age of seventeen," Bernardo exclaimed.

Kylian felt giddy as he left the pitch.

He bounded over to his dad, who was waiting inside the player's tunnel.

"Kylian, Kylian. You'll never guess what you've done … You're Monaco's youngest ever goal scorer!"

Kylian's eyes widened in disbelief as his dad went on.

"You're going to be in the record books for ever now! And guess who held the record before you?"

It occurred to him instantly, and he didn't even have to say the name aloud. He just stared at his dad as the fact sunk in.

He was erasing his hero, Thierry Henry, from the record books, one record at a time.

6
UNDER 19s ON THE UP

July 2016, Voithe-Arena, Heidenheim, Germany
France v England, U19

"I've heard Didier's knocking about somewhere," Jean-Kévin Augustin whispered to Kylian.

It wasn't the first time that day Kylian had heard that Didier Deschamps, the manager of France's senior squad, was coming to visit them. After all, it seemed perfectly plausible.

This year the U19 European Championships were

starting just as the main European Championships ended. It would only be an hour on the France team's plane if he wanted to check out the nation's future talent.

But Kylian was too preoccupied to think any more about Didier Deschamps. He was trying to keep his focus on France's imminent U19s match against England.

Kylian's solid performances for Monaco had attracted attention from national coaches and he was honoured to have been called up to play for the French U19s team.

The honour was all the greater, in fact, because he was the youngest player in the squad.

Being the youngest was nothing new to Kylian, as he'd spent most of his childhood playing with kids older than himself – and he'd always been the best player on the pitch.

He'd been more concerned about the fact that he hadn't known any of the other U19 players in the squad very well, but that had soon changed.

The lads had bonded together quickly in training and he'd particularly gelled with Jean-Kévin. He was from

PSG and had a lethal finish, something that always earned Kylian's respect.

"I told you, didn't I?" Jean-Kévin muttered a few minutes later, tapping Kylian on the shoulder and gesturing towards the tall white-haired man who was walking toward the team.

Deschamps was accompanied by the U19s' coach, Ludovic Batelli, and needed no introduction to the young French men.

"Hi, lads. I just wanted to wish you all good luck before the tournament, and let you know that we will be watching." Deschamps looked at them with a wry grin as he spoke.

There were some nervous chuckles amongst the players as they glanced at each other.

"There is always space in my squad for some young blood," he continued, "so if you do well here, you might find yourself at your next Euros with me!"

Deschamps looked at the faces staring across at him, all wide-eyed and nervous – except for one.

Kylian looked as composed as a seasoned superstar and Deschamps gave the seventeen-year-old a little nod before he departed, sure that he'd be meeting him again before long.

As soon as Deschamps had departed, they turned their attention back to the game at hand. The team had felt strong in training and now, stirred on by Deschamps' surprise visit, they believed they were up to the challenge.

But it soon became clear that that wasn't the case, as they slumped to a disappointing 2-1 defeat against a strong England side.

Kylian was gutted, but so were the other lads, and he felt some obligation to try to lift their spirits. The others were all older than him, it was true, but he was still one of the most experienced players in the squad.

With his encouragement, the whole team pushed themselves in training, trying to improve on all fronts. Kylian was eager to learn all he could from Jean-Kévin, and he shared any tips that would help *him* in return.

Their next game was against Croatia and it was now a 'must-win' if they wanted to go any further in the tournament.

A large group of French fans had made the trip to Germany to watch them play and, from the atmosphere in the stadium, it felt as if they could have been playing in Paris.

France took the lead before half-time, with a thumping finish from Jean-Kévin Augustin.

The second goal came from Kylian. A long ball over the top dropped onto his right foot and he swung at it, hitting it crisply.

At the whistle, Kylian celebrated the victory with Jean-Kévin. Their efforts in training were getting results and the pair were starting to form a deadly partnership.

"Come to Monaco – and me and you can do that all season next year!" Kylian laughed.

"Ah, but then I'd never win anything!" Jean-Kevin joked back.

In the final U19s group game, the pair hammered the Netherlands 5-1 with a hat-trick from Augustin and two goals from Kylian.

"Someone else really needs to score now and then, lads!" Kylian laughed at full time. "Jean-Kévin and I can't keep this up for ever!"

As his friends laughed at his joke, Kylian couldn't help but think he *did* want to do this for ever. Scoring goals for his country was an immense feeling. And knowing that Deschamps was watching only made him more determined.

He needed this man to know what he could do.

The next game was the semi-final against Portugal and France went 1-0 down after only a few minutes. It was a poor start and Kylian could feel the rest of the team looking to him to make a difference.

Picking the ball up on the left-hand side, he walked at the defenders, keeping the ball close to his feet.

Then, with the sudden burst of pace that put fear into the eyes of everybody he played, he flicked it round two of the defenders and swept it into the box. It went to the feet of the onrushing Ludovic Blas, who tucked it under the keeper and into the goal.

"Someone else has scored now!" Blas shouted, as they celebrated.

"Only when I put it on a plate for you," Kylian replied with a smile.

In the second half, Kylian took control again. He scrambled home a cross coming across the face of goal, before flicking a header into the back of the net. It was his first goal from a header, and he was pleased to have finally got one.

"I'm just glad you're using that big head for something useful at last!" Jean-Kévin laughed.

"At least I'm doing *something* – I mean, where were you?" Kylian fired back.

By the time the U19s final came around, Kylian was feeling subdued, knowing that this was the last time he'd be stepping out with the team.

It had been a whirlwind of a tournament and they'd

come so far – they couldn't bear to lose it now. Only one team now stood between them and victory – Italy.

Two first-half goals from Ludovic Blas and Jean-Kévin Augustin put France in control and in the second half they followed it up with two more goals, to seal a 4-0 victory.

Kylian hadn't scored any of their goals and the team-mates he'd grown so close to were quick to remind him of that fact.

"I thought *you* were carrying us, Kylian. Where were your goals?" Augustin laughed, as the boys enjoyed the moment and celebrated their victory.

"Yeah, I was just too tired after getting us all this far! I'm getting old, you know!" Kylian fired back playfully.

The crowd were going wild and Kylian stood back and looked into the sea of faces, soaking in the atmosphere.

When the trophy was presented to the French team he took his turn holding it aloft. He had helped win that trophy and he was hugely proud of what they'd achieved.

As he posed for photographs with the team, he

imagined Deschamps seeing the pictures and writing Kylian's name at the top of his squad list for the senior team.

"Remember this one, lads," Batelli told them afterwards. "There's nothing quite like winning trophies for your country."

Kylian knew what Batelli meant. Over the month of the tournament he'd acquired a taste for playing for France.

But now, he'd acquired a taste for winning with them as well.

7
FALCAO'S FRIEND

August 2016

Monaco Training Ground, Monaco

Kylian returned to the Monaco squad to prepare for the new season with a spring in his step. The success of the summer was still fresh and he was eager to replicate that success with his club side.

There had been several new signings at Monaco and, with a lot of the older players no longer there, they now had one of the youngest squads in Europe.

The club had publicly announced that they were aiming for a top-four place in the league, but their manager had told the team that the plan was really to win the title.

But the season hadn't started the way Kylian had hoped. He'd picked up an injury in training and was spending a lot of time watching from the sidelines.

Although this was a blow, Kylian was mature enough to know that there were always opportunities to learn something, whatever the situation. So he used the time nursing his injury to do just that.

For many years, Falcao had been one of the best strikers in Europe, and he was a lethal finisher in the box. Now Kylian had the time to watch him close-up, and it was a real privilege.

After one match Kylian approached Falcao to ask him why he made the decisions he did – because they always seemed to be so right.

"It's all about watching the opposition, Kylian," Falcao smiled, happy to help the youngster. "If a defender makes a poor touch in the first 10 minutes of the game, then I'm on him for the next 80, ready to pounce on any mistake. They feel that straight away, and that puts even more pressure on them."

Kylian nodded, fascinated by everything Falcao was saying. He'd always been so concentrated on his *own* game he'd never really stopped to think about anyone else's.

"So, just watch the opposition," Falcao continued. "Identify their weaknesses and make them work for you."

It wasn't long before Kylian's injury improved and he had a chance to put Falcao's advice to good use.

He was up front with Falcao against Montpellier and they had just won a penalty. Falcao easily converted it to equalise for Monaco.

As they celebrated the goal, Falcao muttered to Kylian under his breath, "Have you noticed yet? They don't want to head it! Next time Bernardo gets it, tell him to swing a cross in."

So that's exactly what they did. A deep cross from Bernardo Silva came floating over. The defender backed off and didn't go for it, and Kylian leapt powerfully into the air. He flicked it off his head and it sailed into the back of the net.

GOAL!

Kylian celebrated with Falcao as the fans showed their appreciation. Kylian's pace and Falcao's experience were making for a lethal partnership up front – and they were loving every second of it.

As Kylian turned to go back to the half-way line, Falcao called out after him, "Stick with me, kid, and I'll get you 30 goals this season!"

8

LA HAT TRICK

December 2016

Monaco training ground, Monaco

After thirty goals in their first ten games of the season, Monaco had started out with a good run at the top of the table. And even now, at the start of December, they were still second, only a couple of points behind PSG.

Kylian loved to see his club's name right up there with PSG, but he was becoming acutely aware of the price of being on such a strong team.

The reality was that he was struggling to break into a side that also had Falcao, Thomas Lemar and Bernardo Silva, all of whom were currently in great form.

It was something he'd never had a problem with at any of his previous clubs. But here, instead of starting most games, he was only getting 10 or 20 minutes every now and then, and he only had three goals under his belt for the whole of the season so far.

This wasn't the progress Kylian had been hoping for and, for the first time in his life, he had the feeling that he was letting people down.

Sometimes he imagined friends back home watching a Monaco game on TV, muttering at the screen when they saw him just sitting on the bench. Or, he'd suddenly imagine his mum, his fiercest supporter, telling him she regretted saying what she'd said to that Chelsea official all those years ago – he was more of a last-minute sub than a star.

Kylian was always quick to shrug off thoughts like these. He was sure he was good enough to be up front with the other three – he just needed the time on the pitch.

So he decided to speak to a coach about how best to tackle it.

He opted for the best coach he knew – his father.

"Don't be afraid to tell them what you want, Kylian."

It was so comforting to hear his dad's voice on the other end of the phone. He held it as close to his ear as possible, so he wouldn't miss a word.

"But take whatever they give you with a smile – and make that count," his dad continued. "Make it impossible for them *not* to choose you."

Kylian listened carefully. He knew his dad was right.

"It's not their fault that they're not as good a scout as your mum, eh?" his dad went on. "She knew you'd be a star from when you were … "

" … kicking in her belly, I know." Kylian finished the sentence for him, shaking his head as he thought of the number of times he'd heard that one from his parents.

His dad chuckled. "Just know that everyone at home is so proud of you," he added.

A smile spread across Kylian's face. He hadn't realised quite how much he needed to hear that.

The next day Kylian expressed his concerns to Leonardo Jardim, Monaco's manager.

"I just want to play a bit more than the last ten minutes of every game," he said brightly.

"That's fair, Kylian," Leonardo said, listening carefully. "Look, we've got a cup game against Stade Rennais next week. Why don't I give you a start then, and we'll see how you do?"

Kylian was a little disappointed. The cup games were normally played by the B team players, who weren't really seen as part of the main squad. But he stuck by his dad's advice and smiled.

"And if I do well, I'll start in the league – or the Champions League?" Kylian asked.

Leonardo just chuckled. He'd always admired Kylian's confidence.

The game against Stade Rennais was played on a bitterly cold Wednesday evening, and Kylian was grateful he wouldn't be spending 90 minutes freezing on the bench.

With Falcao, Silva and Lemar all missing, the pressure was on him up front and he loved it. He *had* to deliver.

For him, this game was only about one thing – scoring his way into the first team.

Ten minutes in and he was already making an impact. A ball from Gabriel Boschilia was played into space and, even before the defender had turned, Kylian was away, spraying turf up into the air behind him as he raced down on goal.

The keeper came rushing out to close the angle, but Kylian opened up his body and slid the ball into the far corner.

GOAL!

"That was like watching Thierry Henry!" Moutinho roared, as Kylian wheeled away in his celebration.

Exactly 10 minutes later team captain for the night, Nabil Dirar, fizzed a ball across the face of goal. The keeper stuck out a glove and deflected it into the path of Kylian, who had been lurking at the back post.

He slid forward and poked it into the back of the net. GOAL!

Monaco added another before half-time to make it 3-0. And now it wasn't all Kylian – the whole of the Monaco side were starting to run riot.

Half-time in the dressing room, and the whole team chatted away excitedly – all except for Kylian, who remained quietly focused. The game may have been all but won, but he knew he wasn't done yet.

Fifteen minutes into the second half, João Moutinho cut the ball back across the box and Kylian swept it into the net with his left foot.

GOAL!

His team-mates piled on top of him, as they had already done twice that evening.

"He's got his hat-trick, lads!" Moutinho announced to the huddle.

It suddenly dawned on Kylian that this wasn't *just* a hat-trick; it was *his* first hat-trick in professional football.

That was the last of Kylian's goals for the night, but it wasn't the last for Monaco. They added three more before the match ended, to seal a thumping 7-0 win over Stade Rennais and advance to the next round of the cup.

"Kylian!" He heard his manager call him as he walked off the pitch with the match ball under his arm. He turned to face him, a big grin on his face.

"That was good, right?" he smiled.

"Exceptional, Kylian," Leonardo beamed back. "You're making my job of team selection very difficult! I might have to play with six attacking players at this rate!"

Kylian laughed and felt a wave of satisfaction. Tonight, he'd done exactly what he set out to do.

"Did you see that first one, boss?" Kylian continued. "The defender was so far away … "

"Do you know what, Kylian?' his manager interrupted. "I actually preferred the second one. You showed a natural striker's instinct to get on the end of that cross. You can't teach people something like that."

9

THE MIGHT OF MANCHESTER

February 2017, Etihad Stadium, Manchester, England
Monaco v Man City

The draw for the last sixteen of the Champions League pitted Monaco against Manchester City, who were led by the legendary Pep Guardiola.

The news was met with some nerves by most of the Monaco players – after all, Man City were a huge team and this tie would be a real challenge. But the eighteen-year-old in their ranks took the opposite view.

"I can't wait," Kylian had said. "Agüero won't know what's hit him!"

Kylian's optimism soon spread throughout the squad and their preparations for the game began to focus on showing Man City – and the world – how good they were.

Monaco's exceptional form had already put them at the top of the French league this season, and they were also in the French cup final. There was no reason why they couldn't win against City.

"So, what do you reckon?" Kylian asked Falcao as they went to line up in the tunnel.

"Well, they've got some seriously good players in midfield, and we need to focus on getting behind their defence."

Kylian nodded, looking ahead. He'd heard this before – it was similar to the advice Leonardo had given him: "Get in behind Fernandinho and really make him work. You do that and he won't be able to cope with you."

For the first thirty minutes, some of the Monaco players'

initial nerves seemed to have crept back in. City had all of the early possession and quickly took the lead when Leroy Sané squared it for Raheem Sterling to tuck in.

But going one down gave Monaco a new sense of urgency. Minutes later, Fabinho intercepted a short pass from the City keeper and Falcao threw himself at the ball, powering a header into the bottom corner.

Kylian sprinted straight over to him in celebration.

"They're vulnerable, Kylian," shouted Fabinho. "We keep this up and we can win this!"

With only minutes left in the first half, Monaco struck again – exactly in line with Leonardo's pre-game plan.

Fabinho lofted a ball over the top and into the area behind Fernandinho. The City player turned slowly – far too slowly – and Kylian was quickly in behind him.

His first touch took him into the box and, looking up, he had clear sight of the goal. He followed the advice that had never failed him and smashed the ball as hard as he could.

It flew past the keeper and crashed into the back of the net.

GOAL!

Kylian sprinted away to the corner and slid across the slick turf.

He'd scored against Man City.

He'd scored away from home in the Champions League!

It was a crucial moment for him, and he was thrilled to have put Monaco in such a good position, 2-1 up!

Much of the second half passed Kylian by. City dominated the ball and Monaco struggled to get it forward and link up with their attackers.

By the time Kylian was taken off, the score was 4-3 to Man City. Kylian was exhausted and, as he came off, he shook his head at his manager in disbelief.

"I have no idea what's going on, boss," he gasped, as he slumped onto the bench.

"It's a crazy night, huh, Kylian? You've got to love it though."

City ultimately ran out 5-3 winners, but with the second (home) leg looming, Kylian knew it was still all very much to play for.

But an early blow came for Monaco when Falcao was ruled out of the second leg with an injury. He was their leading goal-scorer as well as their captain.

"How on earth are we going to do this without Falcao?" Kylian heard Tiémoué Bakayoko muttering to Bernardo as they lined up before the game.

Kylian had had similar thoughts earlier that day, but he'd since made a pact with himself – he had told himself that he would step up and get them a goal.

It was as simple as that. If he could do it away from home, he could do it at home too.

Monaco went out and attacked Man City from the start. Only eight minutes in, Bernardo Silva dribbled his way into the box and then fizzed a ball across the front of the goal. Kylian nipped in ahead of the defender and poked it into the back of the net.

GOAL!

It was 1-0 already!

"Who needs Falcao when we've got Kylian!" Bernardo screamed to the rest of the team.

The early goal did just what Kylian expected – it gave Monaco a renewed sense of purpose. They continued to attack and Fabinho quickly fired them into a 2-0 lead.

As it stood, with more away goals to their name, Monaco were going to go through to the quarter finals of the Champions League!

Knowing this, the temptation to sit back and defend was strong.

"Lads, we've got to keep pushing forward!" the manager bellowed from the sidelines. "Let's get a third while they're vulnerable!"

But Monaco were struggling to keep the pressure up and they allowed City back into the game when Leroy Sané slammed in a goal.

Now, as it stood, City were going through.

The urgency was back and Monaco started pushing forward again. Focus and effort, keep to the plan.

Minutes later, a free kick from Thomas Lemar found the head of Bakayoko, who made it 3-1.

"I can't keep up with the maths! We *must* be going through now?" Kylian shouted at Bernardo, as they celebrated.

They *were* going through. Ten minutes later, the final

whistle confirmed that Monaco had knocked mighty Man City out of the Champions League.

Kylian looked around at the team that had already achieved so much. Now they were going through to the Champions League quarter-finals.

Grinning at the cheering fans, he simply punched the air.

10
GOING INTERNATIONAL

March 2017

Clairefontaine Academy, Paris, France

Kylian glanced excitedly at the likes of Antoine Griezmann and N'Golo Kanté, who were warming up on the pitch.

When he'd heard he was being called up to the French National Team, he'd been elated.

At club level he still sometimes ended up on the bench, when the other Monaco forwards were selected in preference to him. And yet here he was, selected by the national team coach to play for his country.

It was a huge moment, and he remembered how his dad had actually burst into tears at the news. Kylian understood the feeling. When he'd first pulled his blue shirt over his head, it had brought a lump to his throat.

Growing up, knock-off versions had always been on his birthday and Christmas lists, but now he was wearing the genuine article.

He thought back to how he'd fought for Deschamps's attention last year, when he was in the under-19s squad. Maybe it was his efforts back then that had really earned him this shirt. Or perhaps it was the goals that he was managing to produce under pressure at Monaco that had got him here.

To be honest, none of that really mattered to him now. All that did matter was the simple fact that Didier Deschamps wanted him in the squad, and Kylian now had the opportunity to prove his worth. It wasn't an opportunity he was going to waste.

Fortunately, Kylian wasn't the only Monaco player who'd been called up to the national team. Tiémoué

Bakayoko and Benjamin Mendy had both joined him in the squad and they were welcome companions for Kylian in a France team filled with superstars.

"Don't be nervous, mate," Mendy said to him when they arrived.

"They're the ones who should be nervous!" Bakayoko laughed. "Kylian is going to take their places in the team!"

Kylian smiled gratefully at his team-mates' encouragement and instantly felt more relaxed. Playing for his country had always been the goal – and here he was, ticking it off at barely eighteen years old.

What's more, no one on the team had questioned his presence at all.

Helped by the fact that he was now back within the Clairefontaine grounds he knew so well from his academy days, he was soon very comfortable in their ranks.

"This isn't so bad, huh?" Kylian murmured to Benjamin Mendy, after sending a ball sailing past Hugo Lloris in a training session.

"Wait 'til we're in a proper game, Kylian," Mendy replied. "Let's see if we can still say that then."

The next France game was against Luxembourg in a World Cup qualifier. France were expected to win comfortably against their tiny neighbouring country, and Kylian was desperate to be a major part of the success.

Unfortunately Kylian didn't get to start the game. He had to look on from the bench as Antoine Griezmann and Ousmane Dembélé took up familiar positions out on the wings.

Luxembourg sat deep and defended for most of the first half. The stalemate was finally broken by Olivier Giroud, who fired home a cross from Sidibé out on the right wing to put France in the lead.

But that lead didn't last long, as France gave away a penalty just ten minutes later. Luxembourg slotted it in and levelled the scores.

The Luxembourg fans in the tiny home stadium went crazy as they started to believe that they could pull off a shock victory against their much larger neighbour.

Kylian was about to mutter, "This isn't good ... " to Thomas Lemar, who was sitting next to him on the bench, but he stopped short. Sidibé had been brought down clumsily in the box, and now France had their own penalty.

Griezmann stepped up and buried the ball in the bottom corner. France were now back in the lead.

The second half continued in the same vein, with Luxembourg defending deep and France keeping up the pressure. They were rewarded when the head of Olivier Giroud added a third.

This goal seemed to satisfy Deschamps, signalling perhaps that the game was won. He turned and gestured to Kylian to come down from the bench.

The eighteen-year-old's heart skipped a beat. It was only going to be ten minutes, but he was going to play for his country.

"Right, Kylian," Deschamps said. "They're going to be exhausted now. Get out there and run at them! They won't be able to handle you!" Then he pushed him out onto the pitch to replace Dimitri Payet.

Kylian was excited to do what he'd been told, and to

try to get a run at the Luxembourg defence. He sprinted about the pitch, desperate to get the ball.

Unfortunately for him, the rest of the French team had decided that the game was all but over. They were happy just to hold on to the ball and nobody (except Kylian) appeared to be very keen to look for another goal.

In what seemed like moments the ten minutes were over, the final whistle had blown and Kylian was back in the dressing room.

He was proud that he'd been out there, and he was obviously happy that his country had won.

But he'd been dreaming of this moment over and over in his head for as long as he could remember and unfortunately his first appearance for France hadn't quite lived up to his expectations.

Seeing his look of disappointment, Antoine Griezmann came over to him.

"Don't stress about it, Kylian. That was just the first of many appearances for you. You'll have a hundred caps before long!"

Kylian's next game for France was even more disappointing, as he played for 'only' 60 minutes in a 2-0 defeat against Spain in a friendly.

These had been two tough games in the senior France squad, and neither was in any way how he'd hoped his first matches representing his county would have gone. He'd wanted them to be perfect. He'd wanted a hat trick, or at the very least some assists.

"Play well and there *will* be a next time, Kylian," his dad had reassured him when he'd called him. "It's still an incredible achievement."

Wilfried's words were just what Kylian needed, and he put his disappointment out of his mind.

The next game he was going to play was what mattered now.

As his dad had told him so often, the biggest game is always the next one you'll play.

II
BROS

March 2017
Kylian's family home, Paris

The friendly against Spain had been played in Paris and Kylian was quick to take the opportunity to visit his parents at home.

For as long as he could remember, he had been the promising player who was going to become an elite professional footballer. He loved the expectations and the pressure, and of course he loved the football.

But, deep down, there was nothing more refreshing than going back home and being a normal eighteen-year-old who still got told off for wearing muddy football boots in the house. Just as when he'd been a little boy at Clairefontaine, 'home' was a bolthole from all the craziness.

As he walked into his parents' house this time, he discovered the other reason he loved to come back. It was lying across the sofa, playing FIFA – his younger brother, Ethan.

Now eleven, Ethan shared Kylian's love of football and he was already showing signs of being a promising player in his own right.

"There must be something in the water at the Mbappé house," Kylian's team-mates had joked when he'd showed them a video of Ethan playing.

Ethan's eyes were glued to the TV screen and he didn't even glance at Kylian as he came in.

"Hold on a sec, bro. Let me just wrap up this game," he murmured, still not looking at Kylian.

Kylian slumped down next to him on the sofa, relaxing completely in these familiar surroundings.

He smiled at the fact that Ethan was playing with France against Spain – and was winning comfortably.

Then something suddenly struck him.

"Hey! Hey, Ethan! I'm not in your team! Why aren't I playing?"

He gestured at the screen, pointing to the evidence of Ethan's crime – there was no Mbappé in his squad.

"Just not good enough, bro," Ethan replied, grinning cheekily from ear to ear.

When his game finished at last, Ethan fist-bumped his big brother, making the 'welcome home' official.

"Fancy a game?" Ethan asked, offering Kylian a controller.

"Sure."

They each picked their teams. Kylian went for Real Madrid and Ethan chose Barcelona. Not having played FIFA for quite a while, Kylian was pretty rusty and quickly found himself one down.

"YES!" Ethan cheered.

"Lucky goal," Kylian frowned.

"That's Neymar for you, Kylian. He gets a lot of 'lucky' goals. You'd better get used to that if you want to be playing with the likes of him," Ethan replied matter-of-factly. Then he smirked.

It wasn't long before Ethan scored again, this time with Messi weaving his way through Kylian's Madrid defence.

"Real football is so much easier than this," Kylian moaned, as Ethan made Messi do a dance on the screen to celebrate the screamer he'd just scored.

Suddenly, Ethan turned to Kylian, a curious look on his face. "Kylian, what's *your* celebration going to be?"

Kylian looked at his brother blankly. He couldn't believe he didn't have an answer to the question. It was one that he and the boys at Bondy and Clairefontaine had discussed endlessly.

Back then, it had seemed that a celebration was a must-have requirement for being a footballer. But the last few years had happened in a whirlwind – and he just hadn't thought about it.

"I've got no idea," Kylian replied. "I've been concentrating on getting the goals, you know. Not what I do afterwards."

"Well, you're going to need a cool one if you want

anyone to remember those goals you're working so hard on," Ethan scoffed.

As they carried on playing, they recalled all the famous celebrations made by the great players they loved.

"Oh, and Griezmann does all those dances," Ethan offered.

"Yeah, but Ronaldo's 'Siii!' was always my favourite," Kylian countered.

Ethan knew that Ronaldo had always been his brother's favourite player and, sure enough, he got the feeling that Kylian had started thinking about Ronaldo's great goals. With his brother distracted, he quickly took the opportunity to score yet another on-screen goal.

Ethan turned, as he sometimes did when he beat Kylian at FIFA, folded his arms and tucked his hands under his armpits. His usual grin was replaced with a straight face and he raised his eyebrows and shrugged.

It couldn't have said more clearly – I'm not even trying here.

Watching him, Kylian's face cracked into a wicked smile. He'd just had a great idea.

12

WANTING A WIN

May 2017, Stade Louis II, Monaco
Monaco v Saint-Étienne

When Kylian was reunited with the Monaco squad, they had still been in the race for three separate trophies. But now there was only one that remained within their grasp.

In the final of the Coupe de la Ligue (the French League Cup), PSG had hammered them 4-1.

PSG were the current holders of the trophy and had

won it for the last three years on the trot, so it was a huge ask to expect Monaco to stop them from doing it again, especially with Falcao still missing.

Nevertheless, Monaco had given it everything they had against wave after wave of PSG attack, but it had been of little use.

The result was a huge defeat for the club in what was one of the biggest games of the season.

But what pained Kylian more than anything was the simple fact that they hadn't even been close.

After that game the race for three trophies was over. Now Monaco had only two left to chase.

That changed when they were completely overpowered by Juventus in another 4-1 defeat in the semi-finals of the Champions League.

Kylian had scored the one goal Monaco had managed to get in the game, but he he'd been gutted to see his Champions League dream being dashed as well. With a handful of lethal goals under his belt from the previous few games, he'd really felt in top form – and he'd thought they had a real chance of winning it.

Both losses weighed heavy on Kylian, who was still

unhappy about his two debut games for France. He just wasn't used to this level of failure.

"Do you believe in curses?" he'd asked Bernardo, half-jokingly, in training.

"No, there's no such thing as good or bad luck. I believe that going out and spending millions on your squad wins you games!"

Kylian chuckled, as did some of the other players who overheard the exchange.

It wasn't long before Kylian was channelling his disappointment in one direction – at the last trophy that was still within their reach. A win against Saint-Étienne today would seal the Ligue One title for the club.

Falcao was back from injury and Monaco had their strongest team lined up for the game. It was all looking good.

"I don't need to say anything here, lads," the manager told them in the dressing room. "If you want that trophy, it's there for you. Just go and take it!"

There was a nervous atmosphere in the stadium.

The fans knew what needed to be done, but had the team's confidence taken a hit? Had everyone just got used to seeing PSG winning everything?

There wasn't a lot of belief in the team either, even at this late stage, but that wasn't something that Kylian had picked up on.

As usual, he was completely fixated on one thing – getting the ball into the back of the net. He remembered those wise words from one of his Monaco coaches, back in his younger days.

"In many ways, football is a simple game."

His first chance came in the twentieth minute. Falcao picked up the ball and slipped it into some space down the left-hand side. Immediately Kylian was away, past the Saint-Étienne defenders, opening up his stride and galloping down towards the goal.

The goalkeeper came out, arms wide. Kylian moved as if he was going to curl it into the far corner, but as the keeper dived he carried on running and went straight past him.

Facing an open net, Kylian neatly tucked the ball into the corner.

GOAL!

He'd been running at such a pace that he almost went flying into the barrier, but he managed to swerve and head to the corner flag, where he stopped dead. With a straight face he crossed his arms and shrugged.

Every one of the players from the Monaco team came sprinting up and jumped onto him.

"One chance is all we need, with Kylian up front!" Bernardo laughed.

However the goal failed to kill off Saint-Étienne, and they continued to attack Monaco in force.

There were few chances falling the way of Kylian and Falcao, and they were both taken off before the end, so that Monaco could strengthen their defence.

"Just two more minutes … " Kylian murmured to himself, nervously glancing up at the stadium clock.

"Kylian, look!" Bernardo said, grabbing him. Kylian glanced over at the pitch. Thomas Lemar was in on goal.

"Go on, Thomas!" Kylian shouted, even though he knew there was no way Lemar could hear him. He didn't want to look, but at the same time he couldn't tear his gaze away from his team-mate.

Lemar was now in the box, slipping the ball across for Valère Germain, who slammed it into the back of the net.

Kylian couldn't believe it. It was 2-0 – with only about a minute left! The Ligue One title was coming to Monaco for the first time in 17 years, and he'd played a huge part in making it happen!

At full time all the players piled on to the pitch. Phones were being passed around and Kylian posed for more selfies than he'd ever done before. In the stands hundreds of Monaco flags were being waved by jubilant fans.

"You're a liar, you know," Kylian muttered to Falcao, when the celebrations had started to wind down. Falcao's face wrinkled in confusion as he looked at Kylian's firm features and wondered what terrible thing he had done.

"You promised me 30 goals this season, but I only got 26."

The striker instantly cracked up, remembering the boast he'd made in training last year.

"You're right," Falcao played along. "Only 26 goals, a Ligue One title and two French caps. And all in your first full professional season. You really need to start making some progress!"

13
PSG

August 2017

Monaco training ground, Monaco

Kylian soon learnt that title-winning squads don't always last too long in the world of football. Monaco's squad had been picked apart during the transfer window.

Bernardo Silva and Benjamin Mendy had both left for Man City. Tiémoué Bakayoko had gone to Chelsea, and Nabil Dirar and Valère Germain had also departed.

Monaco had also made some signings of their own, and all-in-all it meant that the club Kylian returned to at the start of the new season didn't feel like much the one he had left.

One morning, whilst Kylian was on a break from training with this new-look squad, his phone rang. It was Wilfried.

"Hey, Dad," Kylian said cheerfully, thinking that his father had just called for an update on all the new players he'd met over the last few weeks.

"Hi, Kylian," Wilfried replied.

Instantly Kylian stopped in his tracks and scuttled into an empty room.

He knew his father well. Just the tone of those two words from his dad was enough to tell him. His dad wasn't calling for a chat. Something was up.

"There's been a transfer offer for you."

"What?" Kylian exclaimed down the line. "Who from? Is it Real Madrid?" he pressed excitedly.

"No. No it's not Real Madrid, I'm afraid."

The pause down the line seemed to last for hours.

"It's PSG."

It hadn't even occurred to him that PSG might want to sign him. It didn't make any sense to Kylian, and for one big reason.

"But didn't they just sign Neymar?" Kylian asked.

"Yes they did, but they want you to play *with* Neymar. Apparently they're building a team to win the Champions League."

Kylian was stunned. To be playing up front with Neymar was something he'd only ever considered when he'd been playing FIFA with Ethan.

"Do Monaco know?" he asked tentatively.

"Yeah," Wilfried replied. "I've spoken to their chairman. He's happy for it to go through, although technically at this stage it can only be a loan. But Kylian, it's going to be about 145 million Euro."

Kylian had no words. He just sat in shocked silence, hearing but not listening to his dad, who had started a long monologue about how amazing this was, how amazing Kylian was, how they'd always known he was going to make it …

Kylian was immersed in his own thoughts, just trying to take it all in.

Then he caught his dad saying the words, "most expensive teenage footballer ever."

Too many thoughts were spinning round in his head. He'd had just one season with Monaco and he was still only eighteen. Making a move like this at this stage of his career was pretty unprecedented.

If he'd heard of a player doing this when he was younger, it would have been a topic of debate with his dad for days.

He could hear it now.

Shouldn't he stay with Monaco and get another season under his belt? Would he get the games at PSG? Should he hold out and try for one of the bigger foreign teams in a few years' time?

But he couldn't fight the feeling of excitement within him.

"Kylian?" His dad continued on the other end, "You still there?"

Kylian responded, his voice cracking slightly, "Er … yeah."

"So what do you think? Do you fancy coming back home to Paris?"

His voice didn't break as he said, "Yes."

After talking to his dad, Kylian thought about how surreal it was that he was going to be lining up with the team he'd played so fiercely against in the Trophée des Champions less than a month ago.

But that was football. And this still felt so right.

The legends who had worn the famous red and blue jersey were many: David Beckham, Zlatan Ibrahimović, Ronaldinho …

And now, Kylian was going to join them.

14
KYLIAN AND NEYMAR

September 2017
PSG training ground, Paris, France

"Looks like we're the new kids," Neymar had said to Kylian when they'd first met.

Kylian had just nodded at him, not sure at first what he could possibly say that would be of interest to this superstar.

But within a few days, the new kids were getting along like a house on fire.

"Next game is against Metz!" Neymar yelled to Kylian. The pair were knocking a ball around, steadily moving further apart so their passes became longer and longer. "Know anything about them?"

"I scored a hat-trick against them last time I played them," Kylian laughed, "So it should be easy for me!"

He flicked the ball into the air and volleyed it back towards Neymar. "You might find it hard, though!" he teased.

Kylian was actually expecting to start on the bench against Metz, given that PSG had players like Draxler, Neymar and Edinson Cavani in the squad. So it came as a pleasant surprise to find himself included in the starting eleven.

As he took his position on the pitch, he was determined that his first PSG game would be one everybody would remember.

However it was the combination of Neymar and Cavani that put the ball away first and neatly handed PSG the lead.

"You're right, Kylian! They *are* easy," Neymar said, holding his hand over his mouth.

But it seemed he'd spoken too soon. Metz pulled a goal back before half-time and, despite their new signings, PSG were struggling to break them down.

That all changed 10 minutes into the second half, when Metz had a man sent off.

Seconds later, the ball was played into the box and was cleared back to Kylian on the edge. It bounced up nicely and he hit it as hard as he could.

It flew past the keeper and smashed the back of the net.

GOAL!

Cool as anything, he'd scored on his debut and put PSG back in the lead.

He ran towards the fans and adopted his now famous arms-crossed celebration. Not only did the pose say, I'm not even trying here, it now also screamed, I was worth every penny.

His overjoyed team-mates piled on top of him, knowing how much this meant, while the crowd chanted his name.

Minutes later, Neymar scored. He burst past a couple of players and curled in a screamer from long range.

"Anything you can do, I can do better!" Neymar joked as they celebrated his goal.

Kylian laughed along with his new friend. He'd never been scared of a little competition.

15

NEVER MEET YOUR HEROES

February 2018, Santiago Bernabéu, Madrid, Spain
PSG v Real Madrid

With the league title all but won for PSG, the club turned their attention to the Champions League. Already, expectations were building.

This was the trophy that Kylian had been brought in to win, and so far all the signs were good. PSG had finished top of their group and had secured a thumping 3-0 win over Bayern Munich in the group stages.

But PSG had never got past the quarter-finals of the Champions League and this year their task wasn't made any easier when they were drawn to face Real Madrid in the second round.

The Spanish team had won this trophy for the past two years running, so a win against them was a huge ask.

Kylian had played in some big stadiums in his career, but they were nothing compared to the experience of playing at the Santiago Bernabéu, Real Madrid's home base.

As kick-off approached, the stadium was a sea of white and the noise of the crowd sounded like thunder, even down in the dressing room.

If this wasn't intimidating enough, Kylian had already spotted some Real Madrid players wandering around in the corridors – Sergio Ramos, Gareth Bale, Karim Benzema, Luka Modric´…

Seeing them in all real life made it feel as if he'd got himself trapped on the wrong side of the TV, in a game with his brother back at home. And this time, Ethan had assembled the best team he could muster.

Then, out on the pitch, Kylian saw *him*. Cristiano Ronaldo – looking as if he'd walked straight out of one of the posters Kylian used to have plastered over his bedroom walls back home.

Ronaldo had been his idol since he was a child and, to Kylian, Ronaldo was everything a great player should be. He stood, mouth open, staring at Cristiano as he came out onto the pitch.

"Oh, a Cristiano fan, are we?" Neymar teased.

Kylian nodded.

"Try not to be too thrown off, Kylian. He's just a guy, you know."

In the match Kylian was up against Marcelo, one of the best left-backs in the world, and Kylian quickly discovered that the Brazilian's reputation was well-deserved.

But Kylian knew that he had his own reputation too, and he was experienced enough now to know that this could affect other players too. So, reputation or not, he just got on with the game.

Half an hour into the game Kylian skipped past Marcelo and fired a ball into the box. It was half-cleared by Real Madrid defender Raphaël Varane, but it fell to PSG's Adrien Rabiot, who slammed it into the top corner.

GOAL!

Kylian celebrated with the rest of the team.

"Let's get them now, whilst they're vulnerable!" he shouted.

He was right. PSG really needed a second goal to kill the game, but unfortunately they couldn't make it happen.

Seconds before half-time, Real Madrid won a penalty. Ronaldo was appointed to take it, and Kylian could only stand and watch as, in a bittersweet moment, his hero smashed it into the goal.

The second half was much the same. PSG had a few opportunities when they were able to break and get at Real Madrid, but they had too little of the ball to do much with it.

With 10 minutes left on the clock, Cristiano Ronaldo struck again. It was 2-1 to Real Madrid.

"Never meet your heroes, huh, Kylian?" Neymar chuckled to him softly, as they jogged back up the pitch.

"2-1 isn't a bad result," Kylian replied. "We're still well in the tie."

But minutes before the end of the game, Marcelo struck a third for Real Madrid.

It was the first time in the game that Marcelo had managed to get past Kylian, but that one chance was all he'd needed.

The second leg went against PSG as well. They slumped to a 2-1 home defeat and come full-time their fate was sealed. They were out of the Champions League.

At the whistle Kylian was gutted to have lost, as always, even though in this case it was against such a strong team as Real Madrid.

But he was also slightly distracted. He was a little overawed – and embarrassed to admit it to himself – but he knew he had to take this opportunity to speak to his hero.

So, as Real Madrid's celebrations were winding down,

Kylian walked over to Cristiano Ronaldo, as calmly as he could manage.

"Well played, Cristiano," he said, trying to sound as normal as possible.

"You too, Kylian. If you're ever coming to Madrid, give me a call, bro," Cristiano replied.

The five-second conversation was one Kylian knew he'd remember for a lifetime.

16
OLD CLUB, NEW TRICKS

March 2018, Nouveau Stade de Bordeaux, Bordeaux, France
PSG v Monaco

"Nothing focuses the mind like the prospect of winning a trophy, right lads?" the PSG manager, Unai Emery, told them as they sat in the dressing room before the game.

It was the Coupe de la Ligue final and, in a weird twist of fate, the game was against Kylian's old club, Monaco.

With Neymar injured, it was going to be up to Kylian to take on a lot of the responsibility for scoring goals against his former club.

It was a strange feeling. Monaco had been his home for many years, but now he was going to try to beat them, using skills that their coaches had taught him. But that didn't mean he was going to pull any punches.

While PSG's Champions League exit against Real Madrid had rocked some of Kylian's team-mates, meeting Ronaldo had put a new spring in his step. And he knew that Ronaldo wouldn't feel bad about beating any of his former clubs.

Besides, if this final was going to be anything like last year's final, then PSG would win comfortably.

Within the first 10 minutes, Kylian created PSG's first chance, twisting and turning his way through the Monaco defence. Then suddenly he felt Kamil Glik sweep his legs from under him, bringing him to the floor.

The ref immediately pointed to the spot, but the Monaco players were protesting loudly.

"I see they taught you how to dive in Paris," Djibril Sidibé said to Kylian, holding his hand over his mouth.

"He clipped me, mate. That's a stonewall pen," Kylian replied, shrugging off his former team-mate's criticisms.

He knew there was no need to argue his point, because – for the first time in French football history – there was VAR and the ref could watch a video replay before making his decision.

As expected, the ref had already drawn a square in the air and had run off to check the replays.

As he came back onto the pitch, he confirmed his initial decision. It was a penalty to PSG.

Edinson Cavani stepped up and slammed the ball past Danijel Subašić in the Monaco goal.

GOAL!

As the game progressed it became clear that Monaco were missing most of their star players from the previous season. They were struggling to get back into the game.

PSG on the other hand were dominant and Kylian was getting a kick out of running at his old team and was creating chances left, right and centre.

One moment he was dribbling the ball into the

midfield, before sending it to the feet of Ángel di María.

GOAL!

The next moment, he was beating his first man and slipping the ball to Edinson Cavani.

GOAL!

At the whistle PSG were comfortable 3-0 winners.

"Disappointed not to have scored, Kylian?" Cavani laughed.

"I set them all up, mate. I don't know what you lot did before I turned up here," Kylian replied with a laugh.

In no time PSG were lifting the trophy.

As the fireworks were set off around them and the fans roared, Kylian hugged his team-mates and took in the scene. The domestic treble was well within their reach this season and, on top of that, there was a World Cup looming.

He was feeling on top of the world.

17
NEXT ON THE LIST

June 2018, Kazan Arena, Kazan, Russia
France v Argentina

On the morning of the match against Argentina, Kylian looked at the little list he was keeping.

1. Australia ✔
2. Peru ✔
3. Denmark ✔
4. Argentina
5. ?

6.   ?

7.   ?

Even though it had been years since the coach at Monaco had told him that football was a simple game, he still liked to lay things out simply – and the World Cup was no exception.

There were only seven games between him and that trophy. Three were already won, so now there were just four games to go.

In reality Kylian knew that Argentina weren't going to be so simple. France may have been one of the favourites to win this tournament, but with the likes of Sergio Agüero, Ángel di María and the formidable Lionel Messi in the team, so were Argentina.

All Kylian knew was he was not ready to go home yet.

He'd been called up to play for his country again, and this was his first major tournament representing France. It was going to be an experience like no other, and he wanted all of it.

The French team had a training camp near Moscow, and the city was alive with fans from every corner of the globe.

"It looks as if the whole world is here," Kylian had murmured to Thomas Lemar, who'd been sitting alongside him on the bus as they'd travelled to their first game against Australia.

"You should have seen it when the Euros were in France, a couple years ago," Paul Pogba had said from the seat in front of them. "The whole country was in one stadium!"

Back on the bus today, Pogba was speaking again, rallying the team.

"We've got to be much better today, guys. Go with pace and power. And stay on them all the time. Don't give them a minute's rest."

Kylian nodded and thought about how good it would feel to tick Argentina off his list tonight.

They were only 10 minutes into the game when Kylian picked up the ball on the half-way line and saw open space ahead of him. He could see the panic in the eyes of the Argentinian defence as he ran at them.

Making it into the box, he spotted the goal in the

corner of his eye and was just about to fire off his shot when he felt a hard shove in his back. It sent him tumbling to the ground.

He instantly looked to the ref, who was already surrounded by French players, appealing on his behalf.

Didier Deschamps, the French manager, had already warned him about this before the game. "You're a danger man now, Kylian," he'd said. "Other managers are telling their players that it's better to foul you than to let you have a chance on goal."

This wasn't the first time it had happened, and no doubt it wouldn't be the last. It was just something you had to learn to deal with, if you were one of the best players in the world.

So Kylian got to his feet, relieved at least to see the ref pointing to the spot.

With this penalty, France had the opportunity to take the lead early in the game – and Griezmann did just that.

GOAL!

Kylian punched the air. If he hadn't been taken down in the box, he might have been the one to get the first goal for France. But this was the World Cup and he was just as happy to be put in the lead by any one of his team-mates.

France tried to hold on to this precious lead as best they could, but Ángel di María soon curled in a stunner from long range to bring the scores level.

Then, minutes into the second half, Argentina took the lead.

"Come on lads," Kylian roared, "we can't let this slip."

But France were struggling to create anything and it looked as if they needed a miracle from somewhere.

As they pushed forward, the ball swung across the box, falling at the feet of French right-back, Benjamin Pavard, who gave them just that. It was one of the goals of the tournament and France were now back level.

Kylian's mind was now clear. They just needed one more. He would get it.

Suddenly, during a scramble in the box, the ball fell to his feet. His first touch took him past the first defender, and his second sent the ball into the back of the net.

GOAL!

France had the lead again! Kylian sprinted to the sidelines and performed his usual sliding celebration, which had become a sensation. The fans went wild and it took everything for him to stop his iconic straight face breaking into the biggest smile.

"Come on Kylian!" Griezmann screamed. "That's more like it!'"

Then, only a few minutes later, Kylian had another. A deft touch from Olivier Giroud and the ball fell to his feet and went whistling past the keeper.

GOAL!

"I think we're through now, mate," Giroud said to him as they high-fived.

Despite a late Argentina goal, he was right and France were into the quarter-finals.

"I'll see you back in Paris when I've got my medal," Kylian chuckled to his PSG team-mate Ángel di María as they embraced after the game.

He was only joking, but he could almost feel the weight of the medal round his neck. Whatever it took, he was going to have ticks all the way down his little list, right up to game number seven – the World Cup Final.

18
THE BOY FROM BONDY'S 100TH

June 2019, Estadi Nacional, Andorra
France v Andorra, Euro 2020 Qualifiers

They were only 10 minutes into the game when the world champions began to flex their muscles.

Griezmann flicked on from the half-way line to Kylian, who then did what he did best. He ran with all his might, suddenly lifting a delicate finish over the onrushing Andorran keeper Josep Gómes.

GOAL!

Seeing the ball in the back of the net was a familiar sight for Kylian, but the feeling that followed was not. He'd already been made aware that a goal from him today on this international stage would be a huge milestone …

This was his hundredth career goal.

As the small crowd applauded his achievement, he let it sink in. He couldn't help but wonder how many goals he'd actually scored in his life so far. There were all the goals during his training at Bondy, then at Clairefontaine. Then, of course, he'd burst into Monaco's team, and then there was his time with PSG, then the national side.

The number of goals must have been in the thousands.

The squad he'd won the World Cup with were now surrounding him to celebrate and their beaming faces reminded him of that last glorious summer in Russia.

As well as being part of the squad that had won the World Cup itself, he'd also been awarded Young Player of the Tournament, and praise had flooded in from all across the football world.

And, as ever, he hadn't crumbled under the pressure of their gaze. He'd only got better, and no doubt he'd just had the best season of his career wearing the number seven shirt at PSG. It was the same number that Ronaldo wore.

The shirt wasn't the only gift from the club either, as his little brother Ethan was now part of their youth team. Perhaps there really was something in the water at the Mbappé home.

"You may have scored four goals in 12 minutes, but I'm going to do five," Ethan would warn him when they next spoke. "And we're not talking about FIFA."

As the team sealed a 4-0 victory over Andorra and all but confirmed their place in the Euros, the twenty-year-old knew one thing.

He felt simply unstoppable.

HOW MANY
HAVE YOU READ?

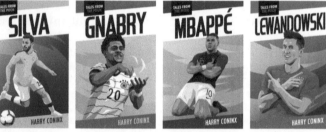